NBA CHAMPIONS: PORTLAND TRAIL BLAZERS

AARON FRISCH

CREATIVE EDUCATION

Published by Creative Education
P.O. Box 227, Mankato, Minnesota 56002
Creative Education is an imprint of The Creative Company
www.thecreativecompany.us

Book and cover design by Blue Design (www.bluedes.com)
Art direction by Rita Marshall
Printed by Corporate Graphics in the United States of America

Photographs by AP Images (Ed Kolenovsky, Gene Puskar), Getty Images (Andrew D. Bernstein/NBAE, Sam Forencich/NBAE, Andy Hayt/Sports Illustrated, Walter Iooss Jr./Sports Illustrated, Layne Murdoch/NBAE, Joe Murphy/NBAE, Panoramic Images)

Copyright © 2012 Creative Education
International copyright reserved in all countries. No part of this book may be reproduced in any form without written permission from the publisher.

Library of Congress Cataloging-in-Publication Data

Frisch, Aaron.
Portland Trail Blazers / by Aaron Frisch.
p. cm. — (NBA champions)
Includes bibliographical references and index.
Summary: A basic introduction to the Portland Trail Blazers professional basketball team, including its formation in 1970, great players such as Bill Walton, championship, and stars of today.
ISBN 978-1-60818-141-4
1. Portland Trail Blazers (Basketball team)—History—Juvenile literature. I. Title.
GV885.52.P67F755 2012
796.323'640979549—dc22   2010052757

CPSIA: 030111 PO1448

First edition
9 8 7 6 5 4 3 2 1

Cover: LaMarcus Aldridge
Page 2: Brandon Roy
Right: Steve Blake (with ball)
Page 6: LaMarcus Aldridge

TABLE OF CONTENTS

Welcome to Portland 9

Trail Blazers History. 11

Why Are They Called the Trail Blazers?. 13

Trail Blazers Facts 16

Trail Blazers Stars. 19

Glossary 24

Index 24

The Trail Blazers are the biggest sports team in Portland

Portland is a city in Oregon. Portland has many trees and flowers. People call it the "City of Roses." It has an **arena** called the Rose Garden that is the home of a basketball team called the Trail Blazers.

Portland was built close to tall mountains and thick forests

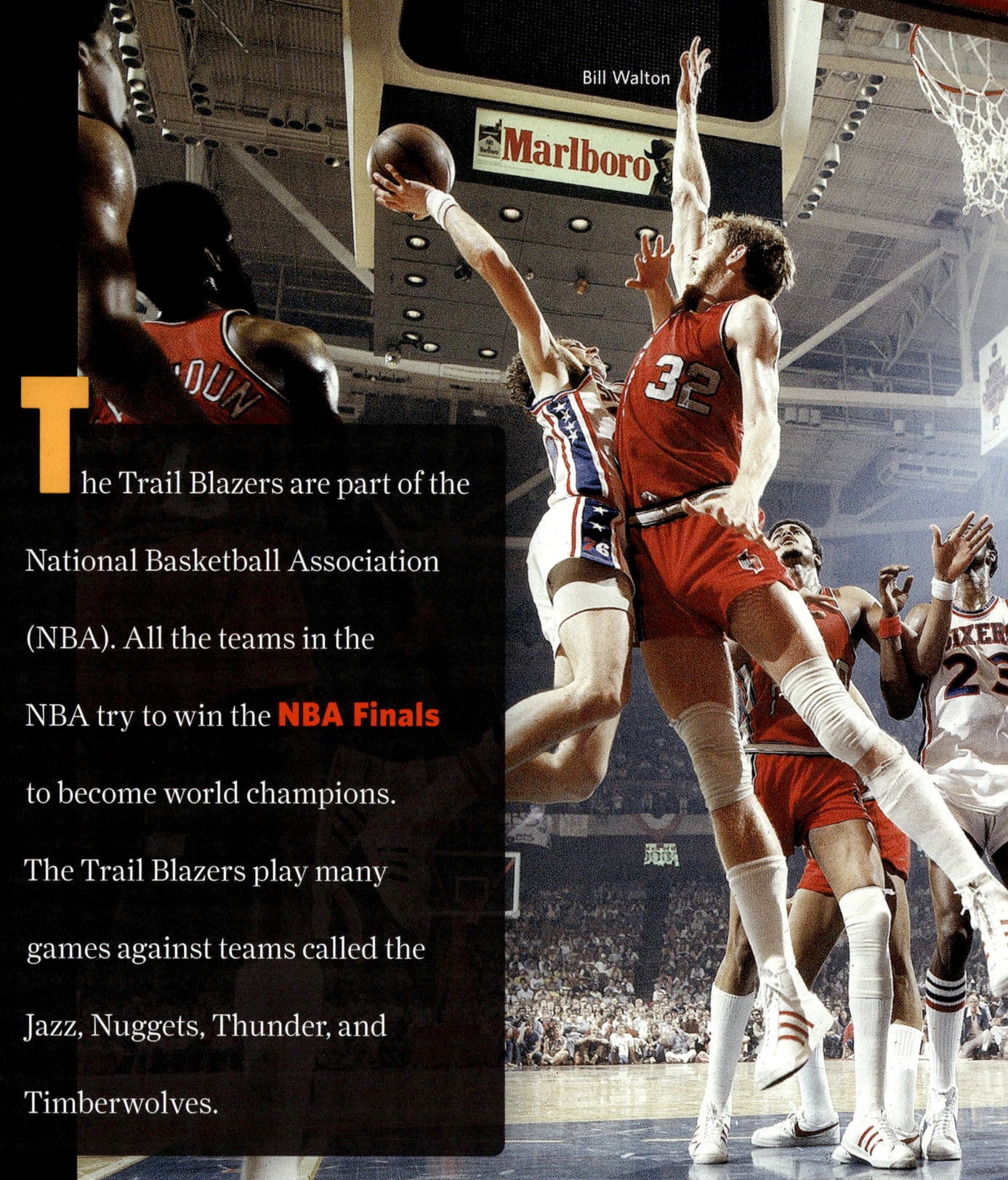

Bill Walton

T he Trail Blazers are part of the National Basketball Association (NBA). All the teams in the NBA try to win the **NBA Finals** to become world champions. The Trail Blazers play many games against teams called the Jazz, Nuggets, Thunder, and Timberwolves.

The Trail Blazers started playing in 1970. They were not a very good team until 1976. That year, they added smart coach Jack Ramsay. They got a tall **rookie** center named Bill Walton, too.

Guard Jim Paxson helped the Trail Blazers win the 1977 championship

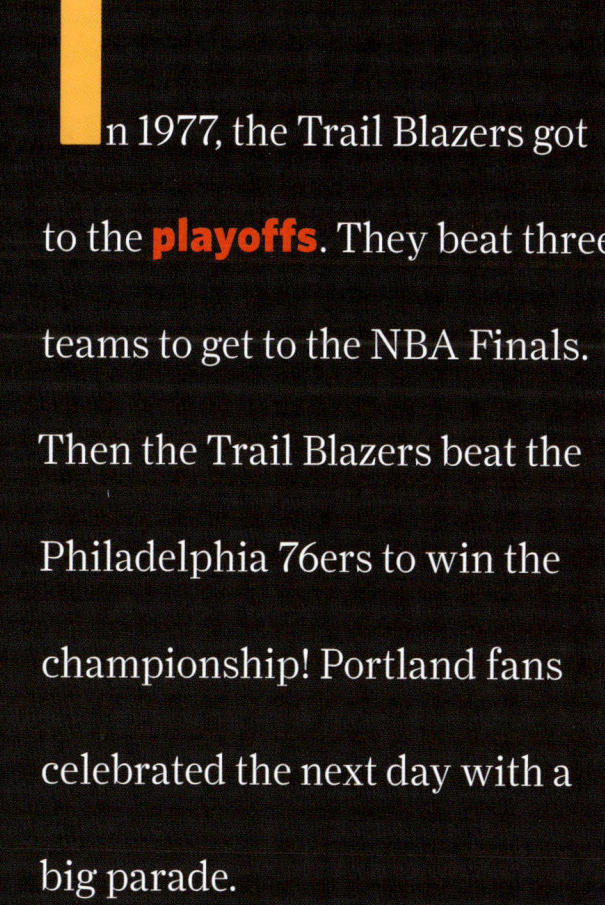

Why Are They Called the Trail Blazers?

In the early 1800s, famous explorers named William Clark and Meriwether Lewis traveled across America to the area that is today Oregon. People said they "blazed a trail."

In 1977, the Trail Blazers got to the **playoffs**. They beat three teams to get to the NBA Finals. Then the Trail Blazers beat the Philadelphia 76ers to win the championship! Portland fans celebrated the next day with a big parade.

NBA CHAMPIONS

14

The Trail Blazers did not win as often in the 1980s. But they became a **contender** again after they added players like point guard Terry Porter. The Trail Blazers got to the NBA Finals in 1990 and 1992. But they lost both times.

Terry Porter (with ball) was a great team leader on the court

Damon Stoudamire

TRAIL BLAZERS FACTS

- Started playing: 1970
- Conference/division: Western Conference, Northwest Division
- Team colors: black, red, and silver
- NBA championship:
  1977 — 4 games to 2 versus Philadelphia 76ers
- NBA Web site for kids: http://www.nba.com/kids/

Portland made the playoffs 18 years in a row. Fans liked watching players like speedy point guard Damon Stoudamire. But the Trail Blazers could not win any more championships.

SAY IT LIKE THIS

Stoudamire
STAH-deh-mire

NBA CHAMPIONS

18

Trail Blazers stars Maurice Lucas (above) and Geoff Petrie (opposite)

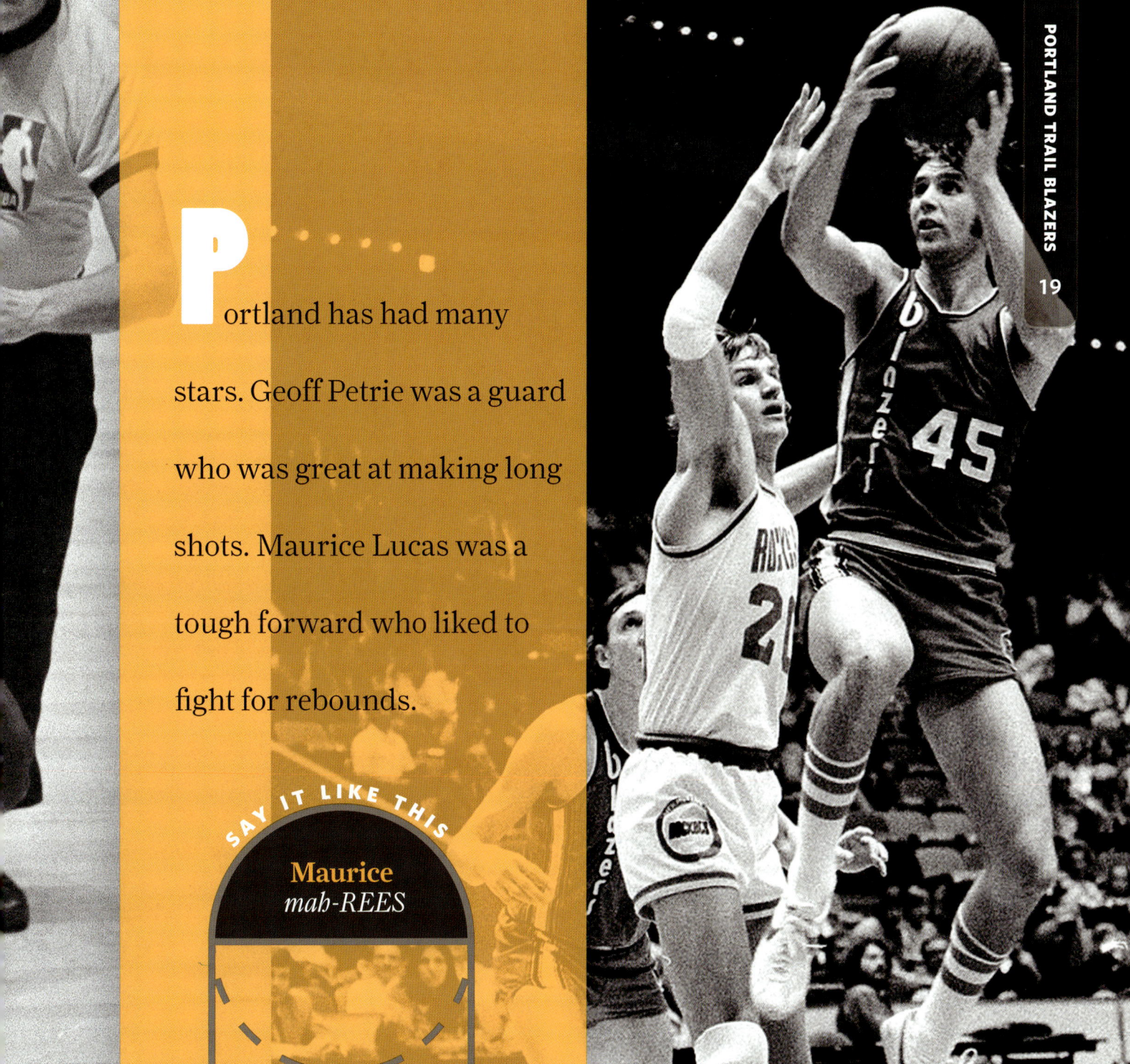

PORTLAND TRAIL BLAZERS

Portland has had many stars. Geoff Petrie was a guard who was great at making long shots. Maurice Lucas was a tough forward who liked to fight for rebounds.

SAY IT LIKE THIS

Maurice
mah-REES

Arvydas Sabonis was one of the NBA's biggest players

Guard Clyde Drexler joined Portland in 1983. He scored many points with exciting slam dunks. Arvydas Sabonis was another star. He was a 7-foot-3 center who could throw fancy passes.

SAY IT LIKE THIS

Arvydas Sabonis
ar-VEE-dus suh-BOH-nis

Fans called high-jumping star Clyde Drexler "Clyde the Glide"

Brandon Roy helped Portland get to the playoffs in 2009, 2010, and 2011

In 2006, the Trail Blazers added fast guard Brandon Roy. In 2008, he scored 52 points in 1 game! Portland fans hoped that he would help lead the Trail Blazers to their second NBA championship!

GLOSSARY

arena — a large building for indoor sports events; it has many seats for fans

contender — a team that has a good chance of winning the championship

NBA Finals — a series of games between two teams at the end of the playoffs; the first team to win four games is the champion

playoffs — games that the best teams play after a season

rookie — a player in his first season

INDEX

Drexler, Clyde 20
Lucas, Maurice 19
NBA championship . . . 13, 16
NBA Finals 10, 13, 14, 16
Petrie, Geoff 19
playoffs 13, 17
Porter, Terry 14
Ramsay, Jack 11
Rose Garden 9
Roy, Brandon 23
Sabonis, Arvydas 20
Stoudamire, Damon 17
team name 13
Walton, Bill 11

Sayville Library
88 Greene Avenue
Sayville, NY 11782

JUL 15 2013

DISCARDED BY
SAYVILLE LIBRARY